WHO IS JESUS CHRIST?

By Pearl Harrington

Copyright © 2019 By Pearl Harrington

WHO IS JESUS CHRIST

By Pearl Harrington

Printed in the United States of America

ISBN 9780578488219

All rights reserved solely by the author. The author guarantees all contents are original and do not infringe upon the legal rights of any other person or work. No part of this book may be reproduced in any form without the permission of the author. The views expressed In this book are not necessarily those of the publisher.

Unless otherwise indicated, Scripture quotations are taken from the New International Version (NIV) . Copyright © 1973, 1978, 1984, 2011 by Biblica, Inc.™. Used by permission. All rights reserved.

www.vinepublishings.com

INTRODUCTION

This book is designed as a children's devotional book for the parents and grandparents who long for their little children to get to know God's character at an early age. They not only desire to teach their children about how to pray to the true living God but also expect their children to have a well-laid and established foundation of prayer life as they grow up.

This book is designed to teach children that it is most important to know as the second person of the Trinity who Jesus is and what He is done for them. It raises awareness of how much Jesus has done on the cross by showing God's love to all. He now is in heaven with God. Because Jesus desires to have a personal relationship with them on earth and in heaven. He is ready to dwell within those precious hearts where rooms are prepared for Him.

Please remember, we as the parents and grandparents sow the seeds. Only God is able to let the truth be sealed and be grown into those precious little hearts.

DEDICATION

This book is dedicated to my own children and the children around the world.

My hope and prayer is that God will open the eyes of children to see Him in person, and their ears to hear His whispering voice. God also will draw their precious hearts to rest upon Him.

Jesus said, "Let the little children come to me, and do not hinder them, for the kingdom of heaven belongs to such as these." (Matthew 19:14)

WHO IS JESUS CHRIST?

1. Exodus 3:14 I am who I am
Dear Lord, You are Yahweh. Thank you for being alive forever! Please open my eyes to see you in person as the divine I AM every day. In Jesus' name: Amen!

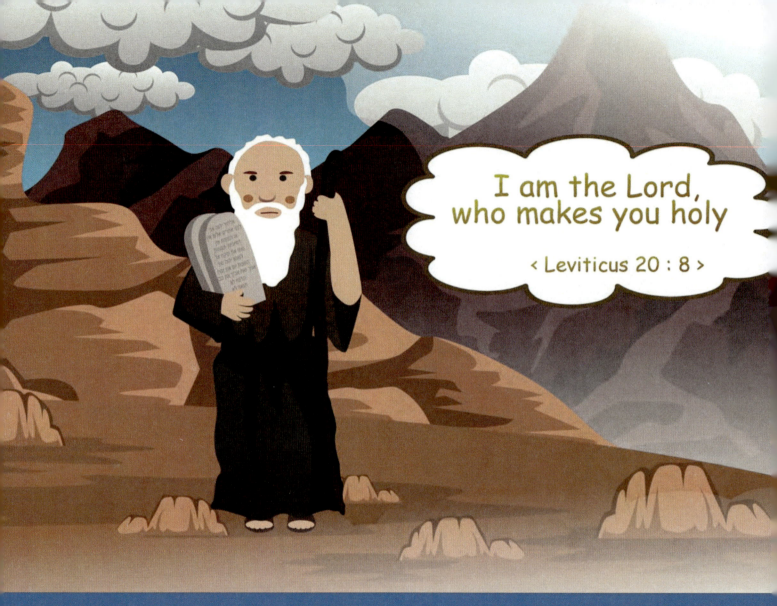

2. Leviticus 20:8   I am the Lord who makes you holy
Dear Lord, You are the Holy One of God. Thank you for always being perfect! Please make my heart pure before you. In Jesus' name: Amen!

3. Isaiah 42:8 I am the Lord; that is my name
Dear Lord, You are Jehovah. Thank you for being who you are! Please make me worship you alone. In Jesus' name: Amen!

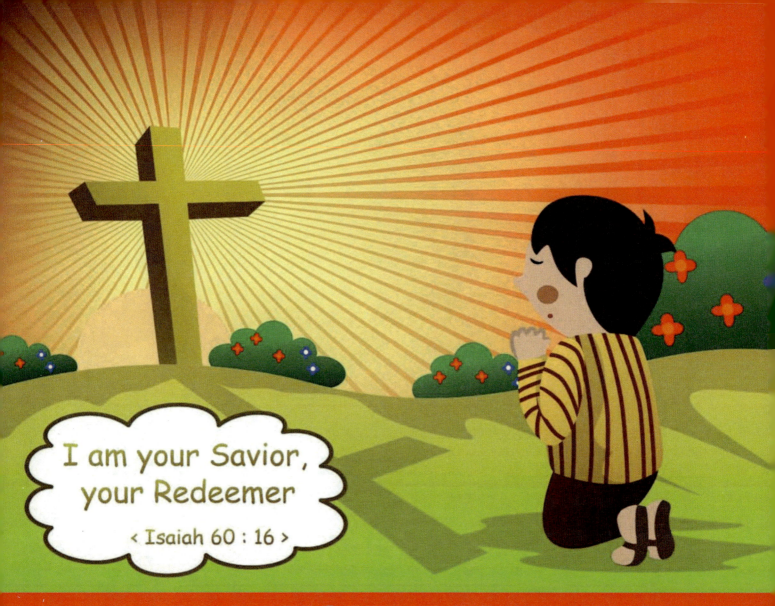

4. Isaiah 60:16 I, the Lord, am your Savior, your Redeemer
Dear Lord, You are the Lamb of God. Thank you for taking my sins away! Please remind me I always need you to save me. In Jesus' name: Amen!

5. John 18:6 I am He
Dear Lord, You are the God who sees me. Thank you for being there for me all the time!
Please have me listen to your whispering voice better. In Jesus' name: Amen!

6. John 6:35 I am the Bread of Life
Dear Lord, You are the bread of God. Thank you for giving me everything I need! Please keep me coming to you for more every day. In Jesus' name: Amen!

7. John 8: 12 I am the Light of the world
Dear Lord, You are the light of life. Thank you for lighting up the world! Please keep me walking with you in the light. In Jesus' name: Amen!

8. John 8:23 I am from above
Dear Lord, You are God Most High. Thank you for your willingness to come down from heaven! Please help me become your good child. In Jesus' name: Amen!

9. John 8:58 Before Abraham was born, I am
Dear Lord, You are the Creator of heaven and earth. Thank you for making everything out of nothing through your Word! Please help me love you more and more. In Jesus' name: Amen!

10. John 10:7 I am the gate for the sheep
Dear Lord, You are the God of all grace. Thank you for being the only gate I may enter through to heaven! Please keep me happy by staying close to you. In Jesus' name: Amen!

I AM THE GOOD SHEPHERD

11. John 10:11 I am the good shepherd
Dear Lord, You are the Chief Shepherd. Thank you for willingly laying down your life for me! Please have me follow you all day long wherever you go. In Jesus' name: Amen!

12. John 10:30 I and the Father are one
Dear Lord, You are the image of God. Thank you for showing God's love to me! Please help me love you with all my heart and my strength! In Jesus' name: Amen!

13. John 10:36 I am God's Son
Dear Lord, You are the Son of God. Thank you for coming down to the earth to do the Father's work! Please help me do good in all that I say and do. In Jesus' name: Amen!

14. John 11:25 I am the resurrection and the life
Dear Lord, You are the resurrected God. Thank you for being almighty by raising the dead alive! Please remind me only you have a superpower to do all things. In Jesus' name: Amen!

15. John 14:6 I am the way and the truth
Dear Lord, You are the God of truth. Thank you for being the only way to get to heaven! Please keep me believing everything you say. In Jesus' name: Amen!

16. John 14:11 I am in the Father and the Father is in Me
Dear Lord, You are the King of glory. Thank you for showing God Yourself! Please keep me to obey you always. In Jesus' name: Amen!

17. John 15:1 I am the true vine
Dear Lord, You are the true Vine. Thank you for taking care of my needs when I need you! Please keep me staying close to you. In Jesus' name: Amen!

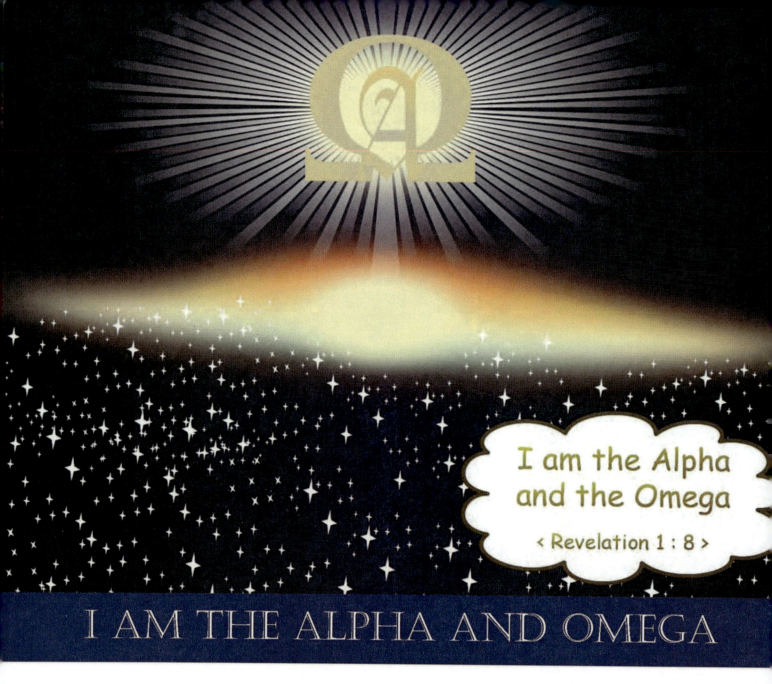

18. Revelation 1:8 I am the Alpha and the Omega
Dear Lord, You are the Beginning and the End. Thank you for being there forever! Please remind me there is no god besides you. In Jesus' name: Amen!

19. Revelation 1:17 I am the First and the Last
Dear Lord, You are the ruler of God's creation. Thank you for making all things new on earth and in heaven! Please help me trust you with all my heart. In Jesus' name: Amen!

20. Revelation 1:18 I am the Living One
Dear Lord, You are the Ancient of Days. Thank you for lasting forever! Please make me true to you always. In Jesus' name: Amen!

21. Revelation 2:23 I am he who searches hearts and minds
Dear Lord, You are the Mind of God. Thank you for being the all-knowing God! Please make my heart and mind pure to you always. In Jesus' name: Amen!

22. Revelation 22:16 I am the Root and the Offspring of David
Dear Lord, You are the Lion of the tribe of Judah. Thank you for coming with a new light! Please get me ready for your return. In Jesus' name: Amen!

Made in the USA
Las Vegas, NV
13 April 2021